Level 1: Beginning to read
Level 2: Beginning to read alone
Level 3: Reading alone
Level 4: Proficient readers

The "normal" age at which
a child begins to read can be
anywhere from three to eight
years old, so these levels are
only a general guideline.

No matter which level you
select, you can be sure that you
are helping your child learn to
read, then read to learn!

LONDON, NEW YORK, MUNICH,
MELBOURNE AND DELHI

Series Editor Deborah Lock
Managing Art Editor Clare Shedden
Senior DTP Designer Almudena Díaz
Production Allison Lenane
Picture Researcher Marie Ortu
Jacket Designer Katy Wall

Reading Consultant
Cliff Moon, M.Ed.

Published in Great Britain by Dorling Kindersley Limited
80 Strand, London, WC2R 0RL

2 4 6 8 10 9 7 5 3 1

A Penguin Company
Copyright © 2005 Dorling Kindersley Limited, London

A CIP record for this book is
available from the British Library.

ISBN 1-4053-0980-6

Colour reproduction by Colourscan, Singapore
Printed and bound in China by L. Rex Printing Co., Ltd.

The publisher would like to thank the following for
their kind permission to reproduce their images:
Position key: a=above; b=bottom, c=centre; l=left; r=right; t=top.
2 Alamy Images: Stock Connection Distribution (br); **Getty
Images:** Dennis O'Clair (tr); **Science Photo Library:** Lea Paterson
(cr). **3 Science Photo Library:** Damien Lovegrove. **4 Ardea.com:**
John Daniels (cl). **6 Corbis:** Kevin Fleming. **9 Alamy Images:**
Natural Visions (main); **Science Photo Library:** David Scharf (tr).
10-11 Photolibrary.com: Leanne Temme. **11 Science Photo
Library:** Damien Lovegrove (t). **12 Science Photo Library:** Gusto
Productions. **13 Science Photo Library:** Gusto Productions. **14-15
Science Photo Library:** Dr. John Brackenbury (background). **15
Alamy Images:** Guy Spangenberg (tr). **16 Science Photo Library:**
Dr. Gopal Murti (tr). **16-17 Corbis:** LWA-Stephen Welstead (b).
20 Science Photo Library: Mark Clarke. **22 Alamy Images:** Jan
Stromme (tr). **26 Warren Photographic. 27 Corbis:** Wally
McNamee (tl); **Science Photo Library:** Lea Paterson (b). **28
Corbis:** Galen Rowell (br). **28-29 Getty Images:** Jim Cummins. **31
Alamy Images:** Ace Stock Limited. **32 Bubbles:** Ian West (tr).

All other images © Dorling Kindersley Limited
For further information see: www.dkimages.com

Discover more at

www.dk.com

![DK] READERS

BEGINNING
2
TO READ ALONE

Sniffles, Sneezes, Hiccups and Coughs

Written by Penny Durant

A Dorling Kindersley Book

Ah -

Ah-choo!
Everyone sneezes –
you and I sneeze, dogs, cats, horses,
turtles, birds and giraffes all sneeze!
Some sneezes are loud but
others are quieter.

Some people sneeze again
and again.
But why do we all sneeze?

And why do we all cough,
hiccup and yawn, too?

choo!

You breathe in the air that
your body needs.
Your nose and mouth are both
passageways for air to get into
your body.
Then the air travels past
your throat and into the airways
that lead to your lungs.
Your diaphragm, chest muscles and
brain work together to keep air
going into and out of your lungs.

Diaphragm
This muscle is springy
like a trampoline.
It pulls down and then
pushes up as you
breathe in and out.

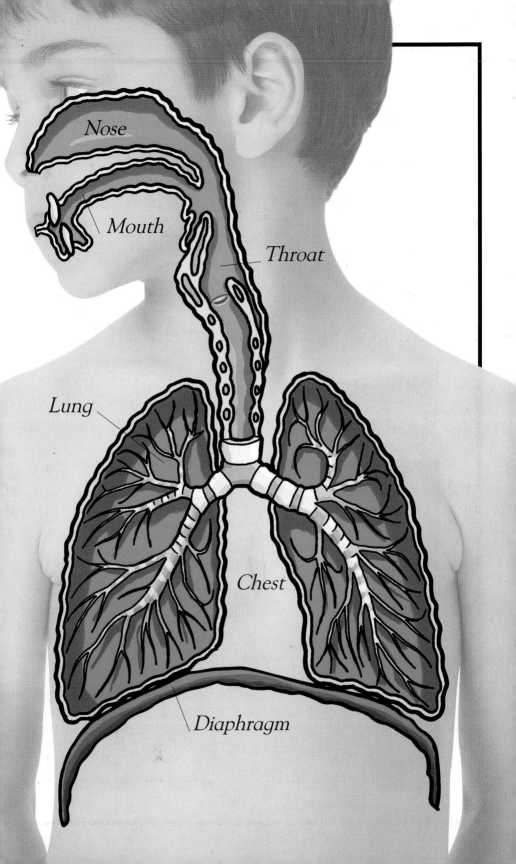

The airways to your lungs need
to be kept clear all the time.
So, when you breathe in through
your nose, your tiny nose hairs
filter the air and the sticky mucus
(snot) collects anything that could
be harmful.
It might be dust or pepper or pollen.

House dust

A speck of dust is not just dirt but a mixture of different things, such as skin flakes, hair, food crumbs and dust mites.

You feel a tickle. Your body does not want these things in your nose. Your brain tells your body to sneeze.

You sneeze most often when you have a cold.
Germs collect in your nose and make it tickle and swell.

Sneezing removes the germs, but they can be spread to other people this way.

Sneezing into a tissue stops the germs from spreading. Some people sneeze when they go out into sunlight. No-one knows why.

Ahhhh...

When you sneeze, you take
a deep breath.
(That is the "ah" part.)
You hold your breath as
your chest muscles tighten.
The pressure of the air in
your lungs increases.
You close your eyes.

...choo!

Your tongue presses against
the roof of your mouth.
Suddenly your breath comes out
fast through your nose.
(That is the "choo" part.)

Your sneeze could be travelling
at a speed of 161 kilometres
(100 miles) per hour!
The gush of air blows
the dust or germs –
and the tickle – out
of your nose.

Let it out!

A sneeze travels as fast as a speeding car, so never try to stop it by holding your nose. The pressure can injure your ears.

Water droplets, mucus, dust and germs are forced out of your nose.

But what happens if the pollen, dust or germs get caught in your throat or airways to your lungs? Then a message is sent to your brain to tell your body to cough.

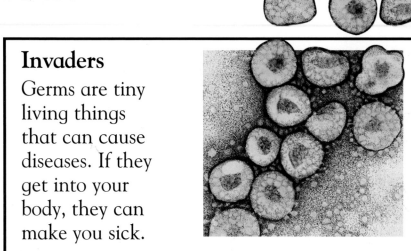

Invaders
Germs are tiny living things that can cause diseases. If they get into your body, they can make you sick.

When you have a cold, you may feel stuffed up with phlegm (FLEM). Phlegm is thick, sticky mucus. It picks up the germs that have reached your lungs and airways. This phlegm needs to be coughed up to clear it out.

Remember to cover your mouth
with your hand when you cough
to stop the germs spreading
to someone else.

*Your vocal cords are
open for breathing.*

When you cough, you take a deep
breath and hold it, whilst your
chest and stomach muscles tighten.

Then your diaphragm pushes
the air out of your lungs.
The sudden gush of air moves
whatever is in your airways and
carries it out of your mouth.
As the air rushes over
your vocal cords, they quiver.

Your cough might
sound like
a dog barking.

Hic. Hic. Hic.

You've got the hiccups.

This may happen if you have

fizzy drinks or you eat too quickly.

Your diaphragm tightens

in a jerky way.

It pulls in sharply and you take

a quick gulp of air.

The vocal cords are closed and

are not ready for the breath.

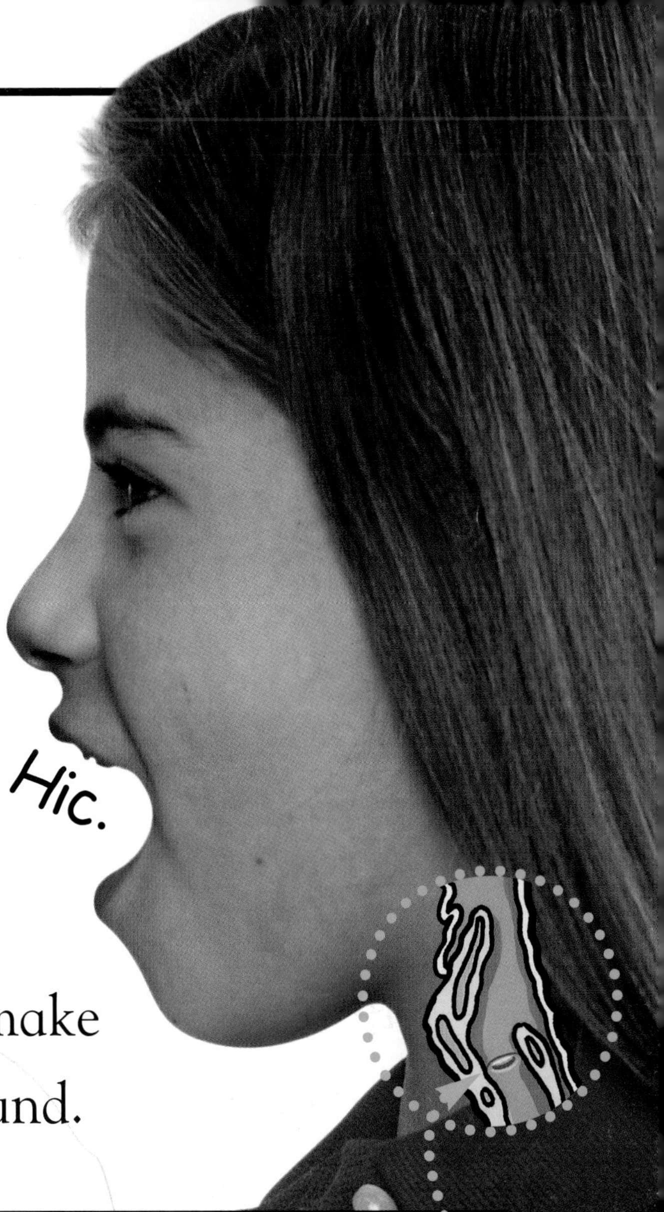

Hic. Hic. Hic.

Instead they make
the hiccup sound.

Voice box

When you want to
talk, your breath
moves over closed
vocal cords, which
vibrate to make sounds.

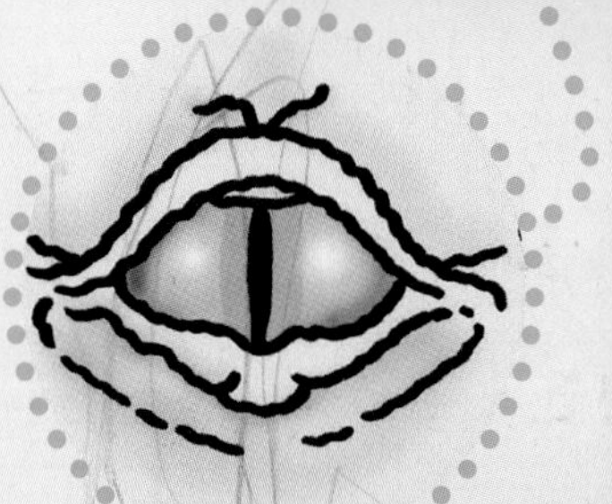

You hiccupped even before you were born. No-one knows why we hiccup, but people try lots of different  ways to get rid of them. Some people hold their breath. Some breathe into and out of a paper bag.

A paper bag can help you control your breathing.

Some people drink water.

Some put sugar on their tongues.

Some people think if you are scared or startled, you will stop hiccupping.

If I yawn, will you yawn?
Probably.
Just thinking about yawning
can make you yawn.
When you yawn,
you open your mouth
very wide.

Your jaw opens
and stretches your face
and neck muscles.
You might close your eyes.
You take in a deep breath
to fill your lungs.
Then you let it out.

Huge yawns
Hippopotamuses
can open their
jaws up to
150 degrees wide.
This is a sign of
warning or anger.

Why do you yawn?
You yawn when you are sleepy,
but also when you wake up.

Warm-up exercise
Athletes yawn before a race.
Musicians yawn before
a concert. Yawning and
stretching make us alert and
ready for something new.

You might yawn if you are bored,
but also when you are not.
Maybe it is a way of saying,
"Let's do something different."

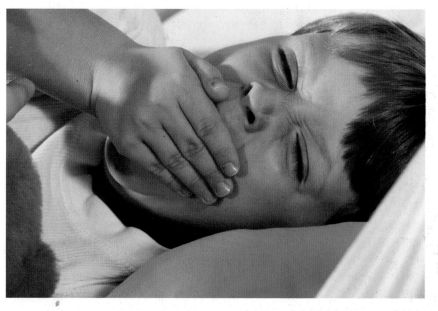

Oxygen is in the air that
you breathe.
Your whole body needs oxygen
to change the food you eat
into energy.
In your lungs, oxygen enters
your bloodstream and then
travels around your body
to where it is needed.
Usually you breathe
without thinking about it.

Breathing out
The air you breathe out
has carbon dioxide that
your body does not need.
Plants use carbon dioxide
to make their food.

However, you breathe more deeply
when you are exercising,
because you need
more oxygen.

Sometimes you may want to control your breath.

You can blow bubbles, pant to cool down or breathe very slowly.

Maybe you can whistle by forcing your breath through the small opening of your lips.

Your body is a marvellous machine.

Remember this the next time
you yawn
or get the hiccups
or cough
or sneeze.
Ah, ah, ah... choo!

Breathing f

We lose half a litre (one pint) of water every day through breathing. We see this water vapour when we breathe onto glass or outside in cold air.

Insects breathe air thro openings in their abdon called spiracles. They h...

Adult bullfrogs breathe in 80 per cent of the air they need through their thin skin.

Some people think that sneezing is a sign of good luck whilst others think of it as a warning of death.

The longest-recorded sneezing fit, lasting 978 days, is held by Donna Griffiths from Worcestershire, UK. At the beginning, she sneezed once every minute.

Charles Osborne from Iowa holds the record for the longest hiccup attack. He hiccupped over 20 times a minute for 68 years – from 1922 until 1990.